Mother To Son

Margaret,

Thanks for being part of the community of women that ensure the success of our youth!

Kevin Crowl
"2010"

Mother To Son

◆

Words of Wisdom, Inspiration, and Hope for Today's Young African-American Men

Kimberley R. Crouch

iUniverse, Inc.
New York Lincoln Shanghai

Mother To Son
Words of Wisdom, Inspiration, and Hope for Today's Young African-American Men

Copyright © 2006 by Kimberley R. Crouch

All rights reserved. No part of this book may be used or reproduced by any means, graphic, electronic, or mechanical, including photocopying, recording, taping or by any information storage retrieval system without the written permission of the publisher except in the case of brief quotations embodied in critical articles and reviews.

iUniverse books may be ordered through booksellers or by contacting:

iUniverse
2021 Pine Lake Road, Suite 100
Lincoln, NE 68512
www.iuniverse.com
1-800-Authors (1-800-288-4677)

The names of people discussed in this book have been changed to protect their identity.

ISBN-13: 978-0-595-39644-3 (pbk)
ISBN-13: 978-0-595-84048-9 (ebk)
ISBN-10: 0-595-39644-5 (pbk)
ISBN-10: 0-595-84048-5 (ebk)

Printed in the United States of America

In memory of my brother, Eugene Rogers, whose ultimate fate I would have given anything to change, but whose death served as the foundation of this book because it helped me realize that I needed to do more.

Mother to Son: Words of Wisdom, Inspiration, and Hope for Today's Young African-American Men

By Kimberley Crouch

Contents

Introduction xiii

For You Are The One xv

Lesson One: Know Your History! You Come from a Line of Kings. 3

Lesson Two: Black Is Beautiful 8

Lesson Three: Black Zombies: Attitude Is Everything 11

Lesson Four: Life Isn't Always Fair—Racism Does Exist 14

Lesson Five: Character And Integrity Matter 21

Lesson Six: You Are Your Brother's Keeper 26

Lesson Seven: The True Measure Of A Man From A Woman's Perspective 29

Lesson Eight: A Penny Saved Is A Penny Earned 32

Lesson Nine: Peer Pressure Will Bankrupt You 36

Lesson Ten: Success Does Not Equal Acting White 39

Lesson Eleven: Put God First 42

Afterword 45

Selected Bibliography 47

Acknowledgments

Sincere thanks go out to my family and friends who have supported me through out this process. It's been a long road, but I appreciate your belief in me and constant encouragement. I especially want to thank my sons, Julius & Justin Crouch, who have taught me the beauty of motherhood, and my husband, Julius, for all his support. Also, a special thanks to Jonna LaGrone-Haynes, without whose assistance this book wouldn't have been possible.

I also want to acknowledge the many of you who were intimately involved in making this book a reality from proofreading to serving as a sounding board. I'm blessed to have had the opportunity to have had your support: Julius Crouch, Sr., Jody Squires, Angel Anderson, Renee Horne, Jill Kvalsvik, Jo Lena Johnson, Laurie Bourgea, Christine Thelander, Alfred Green, Garland Haynes, Stephen Randle, Lisa Cross-Shelton, Devon Adjei, Ann Harmer and Linda Cashdan.

For all those young African-American males who served as inspirations for this book, along with my sons, and whose future I'm invested in, I thank you also: Terrell Ward, Darion Clower, Floyd Hemphill, Terry Parham Jr., Andre Randle, DeAndre Rogers, Gary Rogers, Markel Middlebrook, Solomon Shelton, Dorian Morgan, Jr., Jalen Haynes, Richard Bryant, Jr., Christian Bryant, Gabriel Bryant, Anthony Smith, Stephan Randle, Brandon Childs, Joseph Horne, Ross Golden, and Keenan Squires.

I thank Brenda Hampton and Gail Perry Mason whose own books motivated me to work harder.

Lastly, but most importantly, thank you God for you know my intent and my heart.

Introduction

Growing up, I often heard the adage, "Mothers raise their daughters and love their sons." With the release of movies like *Boyz In The Hood* and *Menance to Society*, this phrase grew in popularity in the African-American community and was often used to explain the social ills that afflicted so many innercity African-American males raised by single mothers. The phrase is founded in the belief that the parent of the same gender is best equipped to teach that child about his or her role in society.

As many children in the African-American community are raised by single moms, the phrase suggests that mothers, the only parent for these kids, cannot teach young boys to be successful men. Therefore, they raise their daughters but can only love their sons. Other than this bleak perspective, not much else is said about the relationship between African-American mothers and their sons.

There is, however, a more positive perspective. As an African-American mother with sons, I believe the mother-son relationship is built on love, respect, admiration, commonality of purpose and uplift. More importantly, it is the source and the foundation from which the African-American race can be elevated.

As a mother, not only do I recognize the special bond between mothers and sons, but I also understand my role in developing and guiding my sons toward becoming productive, progressive African-American men. The results of this mother-son relationship are critical in a society that seems, at times, designed to make them fail and where the African-American woman is often pitted as the enemy.

I also recognize that women are often the primary caregivers to their sons. As such, we are the first women with whom they interact. From us, they learn about gender roles, treatment of women, handling racial adversity and the importance of compassion, integrity and service to mankind. By no means do I intend to imply or assert that the role of the African-American man is not important. Quite the contrary, it is vital. In fact, young boys learn numerous lessons from their fathers that would be difficult for women to teach. This book, however, is about making it clear that there are also lessons African-American women can teach their sons.

In fact, when I look at my sons, I finally get it. I recognize I'm not just raising sons, but I'm also creating pathways for future generations. The lessons instilled in them today could be the very foundation that nurtures the souls and spirits of not only the African-American race but also the human race for generations to come. And nurturing, well now, that truly is the domain of mothers.

For You Are The One

—Angel M. Anderson

For you are the one who was made to lead the way
To break down barriers and form new monuments
So they hover over broad distances as far as the eye can see

For you are the one who was made to achieve
To take hold of your dreams and make new ones
So that you can succeed to the highest degree

For you are the one who was made to live life
To encompass the joys as well as the downfalls
So that challenges are taken with ease

For you are the one who was made to make your mark
To educate generations to follow in your footsteps
So that they can see how powerful of an effect you will leave

For you are the one who was made to have faith
To pass on high morals of nobility
So that your soul can be renewed and set free

For you are the one who was made to be gentle and kind
To possess the quality of virtue and inner peace
So that your rapport with people will help them to believe

For you are the one who was made to conquer all things
To stand tall and strong and hold firm to your position
So that you will follow your own destiny

Mother To Son

For you are the one who was made to endure pain
To appreciate love, devotion and sacrifice
So that your memory will live on and on when you cease

For you are the one who was made as no mistake
To be deliberately placed into your mother's womb
So that you are nourished by the closest thing between you and God

For she gives you guidance, love and support for you to handle
All of the pressures of the world and to give you a know how
On the fundamentals of life for you to achieve anything to the maximum possibility
For all of the times you will need to call on her and for all of the times you cannot
She will be there watching, waiting and praising you as you journey through life.

—Reprinted with the permission of Angel M. Anderson

And so the journey begins

Lesson One:
Know Your History! You Come from a Line of Kings

o o o o o o o o o o o o o o o o o o o o o o o o o o o o o o

If the past has been an obstacle and a burden, knowledge of the past is the safest and the surest emancipation.

—Lord Acton

Dear Kings:

    The Ku Klux Klan once threatened to kill me. They discreetly left a neatly handwritten letter on the windshield of my car when I was in college. It seems they were angered by a speech I had given at a campus event about the importance of black self-determination. In the letter, they threatened to firebomb the apartment complex I lived in or tie me to a tree and give me a good old-fashioned lynching, the kind they say my ancestors received as slaves.

    Oddly enough, the letter didn't startle, scare or even make me tremble. Maybe it was because this was one of several threatening letters I received that year, or because I didn't really believe they would hurt me, or maybe it was simply because I was prepared to die for what I believed in. You see, that was the year I was president of the Legions of Black Collegians, a student organization that served as the voice of African and African-American students at the University of Missouri-Columbia where I attended college.

    While I could not admit it then, I was a bit of a rebel, and the Klan viewed me as a troublemaker, not because of what I said but because of my lack of fear. By that time, I had developed a good sense of self, and people who exude confidence can terrify even the most hateful racist. Confident people also have a sense of calm and peace that they will land on their feet no matter what life throws at them.

I haven't always felt this way. Most of my life, prior to attending college, I felt worthless and didn't see any good prospects for my future. I didn't live in a positive environment, and I didn't see the value African-Americans added to the world. In fact, much of my reality involved African-Americans engaged in killing, stealing and drug-dealing. The only thing I ever learned in school or on television about African-American people was that we had been slaves, a lot of us were on welfare and we would kill our own as easily as water flowed from a faucet. Also, Africa was seen as a backward continent where people danced around naked all day, carried fruit on their heads and had no education or culture.

I am embarrased to admit it now, but back then, I hated being African-American. I wanted no part of any race that seemed to add little value to our society, and I spent a good deal of my adolescent years holding my head down in shame. Everywhere I went, I pretended to be someone or something I wasn't. I told people my father was a white guy from England and that I lived in an affluent neighborhood. I insisted on this, even though my complexion made it obvious to everyone that my father was anything but white, and my clothes portrayed anything but class or money. I did anything and everything not to be associated with my race.

My greatest regret about my childhood is that I spent most of it denying the essence of who I was and not appreciating my heritage. Unfortunately, I wasn't alone. Lots of young African-American children felt the same way because everything from the school system to television had taught us to view ourselves this way from the day we were born.

However, my self-hate and perceptions changed during my freshman year of college when I attended a seminar by an excellent orator and intellectual, Jawanza Kunjufu, who had written several books geared toward the uplift of African-Americans. During the seminar, he stressed the importance of knowledge and educated us on the enormous contributions of Africans and African-Americans that I had never heard before. When he finished, my entire view of Africa, the African-American race and, ultimately, my self had changed.

These stories and facts taught me that I had value and that my race had actually played an important role, not only in its contributions to America's history but also to the world's history. This is an easy thing to say but truly a hard concept to grasp if you're a child and your entire world, whether in reality or on television, is filled with negative images of African-Americans. It's hard to live life never seeing anything of value attributed to your race. At that point in my life, I thought every other race had something, even if it was a stereotype, of which to be proud. Whites were thought of as the founders of civilization who had brought the concepts of the written word and math to the world. Asians were seen as smart; Jewish people were known as God's chosen people; and Hispanics were judged by the great civiliations of the Aztecs and Mayan Indians.

As a child, I lacked the knowledge of history that I have now. I've come to realize that, with regard to history, the dominant race often places greater emphasis on its contributions while minimizing the contributions of others. This is why I know the most valuable lesson I can teach you is about your heritage. A child with a strong sense of heritage is instantly validated by himself or herself and doesn't need to look for that validation in unwise places. I know from experience that you will hear little on television or in school about the contributions of Africans or African-Americans. Although nowadays you do hear a lot about Tiger Woods, Serena Williams and LeBron James, I want you to know there is so much more to the African-American race than excellence in sports. Truth is, you come from Africa, the birthplace of great kings and queens.

Today, it is almost without dispute that Africa was the origin of civilization. It thrived as a prosperous continent thousands of years ago. It was the continent of prestige and growth, commerce and education. For centuries, and even into modern times, many great kings and queens ruled such as:

> Taharqa, King of Egypt and a member of the Nubian Dynasty, who ruled Egypt during the 25th Dynasty (690–664 B.C.). He was one of the greatest of the Nubian pharoahs. He engaged in many battles with and helped Israel in their resistance against the invading Assyrians. He is mentioned in the Bible as the King of Ethiopia (also known as Nubia)(Isaiah 37:9, 2 Kings 19:9). During his reign, he controlled the largest empire in ancient Africa. He was also a prolific builder and responsible for numerous construction projects included rebuilding of the temple at Kawa and restoration of the temple at Karnak. He is also believed responsible for the building of the temple at Gebel Barkal in the Sudan.

> Tiye, the Nubian Queen of Egypt. Queen Tiye was the wife of Amenhotep III, a pharaoh from the 18th Dynasty. She enjoyed great power during her husband's reign and served as his trusted advisor. She is the first queen of Egypt to have her name on official acts. Amenhotep viewed her as his equal and sought her advice on political, foreign and military matters, and he built numerous temples and statutes in her honor. Her son, Akhenaten, a powerful king in his own right, is believed by some scholars to be the father of King Tutankhamen, also known as King Tut.

> Nzingha, Amazon Queen of Matamba, West Africa (1582–1663). Nzingha was an Angolan queen who excelled as a military leader. She was a

fierce military strategist and diplomat who fought the Portuguese for many years to keep her people free from slavery. She allied her nation with the Dutch to fight the Portuguese, marking the first African-European alliance against a European oppressor. Even after being forced into exiled, Nzingha continued to wield considerable influence among her people because of her efforts to keep them free.

In addition to the great kings and queens of Africa, here are a few other things you may not hear at some point in your life. I include them here because they clearly underscore the richness of the contributions of Africans and African-Americans:

Egypt and not Greece was the origin of civilization.

Philosophers, Socrates and Plato, got their philosophical teachings from African philosophers such as Ptahhotep and Akhenaten.

Imhotep and not Hippocrates was the real Father of Medicine. Imhotep is recognized as the world's first physician and lived during the Third Dynasty at the court of King Djoser. It is believed he built the first pyramid, the step pyramid of Saqqara. Imhotep is credited with treating such diseases as tuberculosis, gallstones, appendicitis, gout and arthritis. His teachings were assimilated into Greek culture. Hippocrates, who became known as the Father of Medicine, actually lived 2,000 years after him.

Louis Howard Latimer is credited with drafting Alexander Graham Bell's telephone patents.

Dr. Walter McAfee, an African-American astrophysicist, played a vital role in helping to usher in the start of the Space Age. Dr. McAfee was part of a team of scientist involved in Project Diana, a US Army Program, in the 1940s that was responsible for the first radar lunar echo experiments. Dr. McAfee performed the mathematical calculations that made it possible for the scientist to bounce radar signals off the surface of the moon. Dr. McAfee's name and contributions were never mentioned when news announcing this historic occassion was released. Even so, his contributions helped to shepard in a new era of space exploration.

Mary Elizabeth Bowser, a former slave, served as part of a Union spy ring while working as a household servant in the home of Jefferson Davis, the Confederate President. Davis was unaware that Bowser had been educated, and she used his lack of this knowledge to her advantage. Her duties allowed her access to Davis's study where she was able to read war dispatches and his private papers, and he openly spoke about war matters in her presence. She was never caught and continued her work on the Union's behalf for the duration of the war. African-American spies, such as Bowser, who provided intelligence on Confederate forces to the Union were known as black dispatches, and they played an important role in helping the Union win the Civil War.

The list of contributions could go on, but suffice it to say, as you journey throughout your life, I want you to hold your head high and think of all the greatness associated with your culture. Don't be swayed by the fact that you may never hear about this history except at home. Napoleon Bonaparte got it right when he said, "History is the version of past events that people have decided to agree upon." So as long as you know your heritage, you will always know the truth and be able to hold your head high. It's hard to make men, or women for that matter, feel inferior when they know they come from greatness.

So if you never hear this from the world at large, I want you to hear from me and remember forever that you are kings! Most importantly, you don't have value because you are kings, but you are kings because you have value.

Love Mom,

Mother of Kings

Lesson Two:
Black Is Beautiful

Beauty is an experience, nothing else. It is not a fixed pattern or an arrangement of features. It is something felt, a glow or a communicated sense of fineness. What ails us is that our sense of beauty is so bruised and blunted, we miss all the best.

—D. H. Lawrence

Dear Tall, Dark and Handsomes:

Your Aunt Deborah and cousin Sherry came to visit today. We played games, talked about old times and even watched a few movies. Things were going pretty well until Sherry asked for a bowl of Lucky Charms cereal. This should have been an easy exercise, right? Well it wasn't. As soon as I handed Sherry the black bowl to eat her cereal, she completely lost control. She started crying, told me she was white, not black, and refused to eat the cereal out of the black bowl.

This concerned me because I had never seen a seven-year-old become despondent over the color of a bowl. After all, I thought most children cared only about the type of cereal they ate, not the bowl they ate it from. But Sherry has always been strange. Nevertheless, I asked what was wrong with the black bowl. Sherry told me she didn't find the color black attractive and she had no intention of being black or using something black. What's worse, she stated she wanted to be white like me. This stunned me because I had definitely overcome my self-hatred and definitely knew I was African-American and proud to be so.

After spending almost an hour with Sherry, I realized she thought that African-Americans with light complexions were white. More importantly, I realized she suffered from the same self-hatred I had, but hers had started at a much younger age. She told me that although her mom was black, she had no intention of being black and didn't like black people. I spent most of the day trying to help Sherry see and understand the beauty of her blackness. While it took me a long time to eventually convince her that black was beautiful, I clearly understood her rationale.

Growing up, I always dreamed of being beautiful. It's not that anyone ever told me I was ugly. Rather, I learned from television and society that women who looked like me—African-Americans, with full lips and curvy hips—weren't beautiful. I also associated "good hair and pretty eyes" with being white. Sherry, like myself, had internalized these societal images of beauty. Who could blame her? After all, you seldom saw African-Americans depicted on television or in magazines as beautiful.

Over time, I learned that beauty epitomized more than a physical notion. It was also a spiritual notion, stemming from what's on the inside just as much as what is visible on the outside. This is true even though the world is full of images that make you think differently. The concept of beauty is culturally constructed and varies both with geography and time. In American society, the standard of beauty is often judged as that of white women, particularly those with the coveted blonde hair and blue eyes, who are as thin as a pencil.

This standard somehow has been transferred and personified tenfold in the African-American community, which has attached its own internal cultural hierarchy to beauty. The closer you are to that American societal standard, the more beautiful you are deemed. For example, those African-Americans who are light-complected with long hair are often viewed as more beautiful than a dark-skinned sister with short hair. I admit it took me a long time to be proud to be black; but once I was, there was no stopping me. For black is beautiful, and I came to appreciate this slogan, created by our ancestors to reclaim not only their heritage but their self-esteem and the self-esteem of their children.

Since that time, I have attempted to reclaim my blackness and recognize the infinite beauty of it. Vanilla, chocolate, caramel, hot fudge...we come in all colors, and although the phrase "black is beautiful" is popular, the term "black" doesn't really come close to describing the variety that exists among us African-Americans, Afro Americans or, yes, black folk. We are a part of our own rainbow of colors. Our race is so beautiful—our broad noses, thick lips, wooly hair, hips out to there...I could go on.

We can be called many things, but plain is not one of them. Even to this day, I continue to embrace my "blackness" in new ways. Whether I do so by adopting certain practices or just by embracing my own natural hair, I'm learning to have a greater appreciation for us as a people. I'm learning to be more comfortable with myself and all the things that make me great.

I hope you learn these lessons far sooner than I did because it will affect the journey you take, your outlook on life, the decisions you make, your responses to obstacles that come your way and ultimately the legacy you will leave behind. Most importantly, it may affect the women you date and the spouse you select, because society will constantly steer you toward beauty as defined by that of a white woman. This doesn't mean that white women aren't beautiful. It's just that I don't want you to forget the beauty of African-American women, which may be hard to remember in a world constantly bombarding you with the message that women in your own race aren't beautiful. This is why I tell you there's so much beauty in the African-American race.

So say it loud, "You're black and you're proud," and remember always that black truly is beautiful and so are you.

Love Mom,

Woman Who Wants You To Know You're Beautiful

Lesson Three:
Black Zombies: Attitude Is Everything

o o o o o o o o o o o o o o o o o o o o o o o o o o o o o o

The greatest discovery of my generation is that human beings can alter their lives by altering their attitudes of mind.

—William James

There are no broken dreams, only broken spirits.

—Matt Luders

A successful man is one who can lay a firm foundation with the bricks others have thrown at him.

—David Brinkley

Dear Eternal Optimists:

I recently travelled back to St. Louis and witnessed my first Cardinals baseball game in nearly 10 years. Although they lost 8–1, it was good to see the old team live at Busch Stadium. Perhaps the best part of the trip involved going through my old neighborhood again: the Walnut Park Area. We, St. Louisians, know this section of town has evolved into a do-or-die area because of the struggle and peril that many African-American youth face while growing up here. It is truly a case study of the survival of the fittest, nature at its rawest. I hadn't been back to this area since my brother died in 1996 because I still harbored lots of ill will that someone callously murdered him in the very neighborhood we once affectionately called home.

Despite attempts to revitalize St. Louis, the Walnut Park area has virtually remained in a state of decay. It was, however, nice conversing with some of my old friends who still lived in the neighborhood and even to walk the streets again without fear like I had done as a child. In an odd sort of way, it was refreshing to be back in the old digs, listening to the conversations amongst my old friends, and the men and women on the streets. Unfortunately, people living there have a grim outlook, both on their chances for survival and their chances of getting out of the slums. They seemed despondent, with a lot of hopelessness and misguided focus.

I started reminscing about my childhood and about how we, as kids, had so many dreams and plans for the future. Many of the friends I visited with today once wanted to be doctors, lawyers, actresses and business owners—one even wanted to be an astronaut. With the exception of a few of us, the rest never realized their dreams. Many died before they graduated from high school. Those who didn't, well, let's just say their bodies are here, but their souls died years ago.

I started thinking about a song by the rapper Nas, *Black Zombie*, as it reminded me of the mental state of the kids I passed in the streets that day and of the friends I had known since childhood. I suppose it's understandable that positiveness is in short supply, considering that the unemployment rate is high, black-on-black crime remains rampant and our people seem to have no vision or direction. I wonder what will become of our youth. Clearly, the problem is systemic and not limited to Walnut Park or St. Louis. I can go to any slum in the North, South or on the East, Central or West coasts and see the same condition. People seem unable to grasp control of their future, stand with strength and refuse to fail. Such hopelessness clearly illustrates how attitudes and perceptions determine a person's success or failure.

I want you to realize that throughout your life, you will encounter people who appear to have everything: wealth, a successful career, a luxurious home, a supportive spouse and adoring kids. You will ask yourself the same questions everyone asks: is it family background, inherited wealth, education, or simply luck? Or is success predetermined by nature? While I do believe these factors play some role, I believe the greatest factor is a person's attitude, in perception of and response to life.

In fact, I've come to realize that attitude is more important than your past, your birth order, your family circumstances, your education and your socioeconomic status. To me, attitude is the greatest equalizer, and it can can make or break a company, a career, a marriage, or you. I acknowledge that you cannot change your past, your race, the family you were born into or how people behave toward you. You simply have no control over these things. However, the one thing you can change and control is your attitude in how you see yourself, the world around you and the circumstances you encounter.

People often question how two kids born into a bad situation, with the same parents and who are raised similarly, turn out differently. For me, there's a simple explanation. Two people, everything else being equal, can have different reactions to the same set of stimuli (in this case, the stimuli are environment and family circumstances). It all comes down to perception and attitude. At the end of the day, I believe your attitude matters more than anything else.

Some people adjust to difficult circumstances, while others totally reject them. Those who adjust allow the poor family circumstances and environment to destroy their beliefs, hopes, desires and dreams. Those who reject it use the circumstances and environment to propel themselves to greater heights. In the end, attitude and perception are the biggest differences.

Only you can control whether you see the glass as half empty or half full. Only you control whether you see America as a land of opportunity or as a country designed to make African-Americans fail…whether you see the world as giving you a hand up or a hand down…whether you see a world full of racists or full of nice people.

While I want you to look at life realistically—racism does exist, after all—I want you to understand the role your attitude plays in determining your response to situations. This is true no matter what the world throws at you, no matter how much you think the world is against you (and at times you will think this) and no matter how much you question the opportunities in this world for African-American men or African-Americans in general.

If you ever lose your way, remember these two things:

You come from the birthplace of kings and queens, and no one can ever take that from you.

Your reality is based on your perception, so if necessary, change your perception.

Find the lesson in whatever ails you, adjust your attitude and keep forging ahead. In the end, I say, choose to see the beauty of life or forever stay among the walking dead.

Love Mummy,

Your Guardian Angel

Lesson Four:
Life Isn't Always Fair—Racism Does Exist

o o o o o o o o o o o o o o o o o o o o o o o o o o o o o o o

Racism is man's gravest threat to man—the maximum of hatred for a minimum of reason.

—Abraham Joshua Heschel

We can go on talking about racism and who treated whom badly, but what are you going to do about it? Are you going to wallow in that or are you going to create your own agenda?

—Judith Jamison

Dear Men of Justice:

At seven years of age, I learned I was a nigger. Funny thing is, I didn't learn it from a white person, but from my childhood friend, Ava Johnson. She told me that she and her mom had gone shopping at a mall in a rich white neighborhood and a white man had told her and her mom to leave because they didn't want any niggers around that part of town. Although neither Ava nor I knew what it meant to be a nigger, we both knew, because the man had yelled and shouted it, that it wasn't a compliment.

Later that night, I asked my grandmother what the word meant. The way she looked at me told me I should never repeat it in her presence again. Even so, she explained that the word had often been used by people of other races to insult African-American people with the intent to make them feel inferior. She told me that if someone ever called me that word, it was more a reflection of their ignorance and intolerance, and that I should simply ignore it. Although I had lots of questions, my grandmother's face told me she had explained more than she cared to and to leave the situation alone.

Over the years, I have had my own experiences with the word. As I grew older, I learned about racism in America, and the evil and contempt that bred such hatred. According to the Merriam-Webster dictionary, racism is defined as the belief that race is the primary determinant of human traits and capacities and that racial differences produce an inherent superiority of a particular race. Racism, in America at least, has often been used by individuals in the dominant race to discriminate or mistreat African-Americans and other people of color.

From slavery to Jim Crow laws to corporate America today, America's legacy of racism in its institutional systems and culture has been clearly documented. It is a legacy without dispute or question. In spite of this, America undeniably remains the best country on earth to make your home. America is also the land of opportunity and hope, and the one place you can make any dream you have come true, so long as you are persistent, remain committed and don't get discouraged. But discouraged you will be.

As African-American men, it's important that you recognize upfront that life is unfair, but its unfairness is not irrevocable. In spite of the unfairness, you have the capacity to prevail, because you have a strong sense of self and a belief in your capabilities. This doesn't mean racism is right or that you should accept it. Quite the contrary, it means I want you to acknowledge upfront that racism exists. This way you can recognize it, confront it, when appropriate, and do what you can to level the playing field for future generations of African-Americans. However, do not, and I repeat, do not allow the racists out there to define you. You see, it's easy to get caught in the trap of expending lots of energy trying to understand why things aren't fair, or remaining stifled because they aren't fair.

Additionally, it's easy to lose hope once you realize that those in power sometimes make decisions based on things like your skin color, even though society espouses the principle that merit and hard work are all that matters. To a great many people in the world, skin color does matter, even if you hear something to the contrary. However, you have nothing to be ashamed of in being African-American, because you come from a rich heritage of greatness and you're beautiful, and no one can change that.

Even so, life remains unfair, and the automatic reaction to such unfairness for most people is anger and resentment. You will inevitably encounter unfairness as you grow up. Your reactions to that will determine the kind of person you become as an adult and ultimately whether or not you become a contributor to society. The most important thing for me is whether I teach you, and you learn, the difference between actual victimization, which must be confronted on every occasion, and submitting to the belief that you are a victim and are helpless to change the situation.

This is why I want you guys to accept that life is unfair upfront and look inward to your internal strength and courage to address life's inequities. Remember, no one ever promised any of us a life free from pain and disappointment, even if unwarranted. Truthfully, life is full of unfairness, and it's better that you understand this reality. This explains why some people are born poor and others wealthy; some born with diseases and others healthy; some born with limbs and others aren't or are born deaf, blind or with other handicaps; some are born great singers and others great artists; some are born with high intelligence and others are mentally challenged. This explains why someone of immense faith and belief in God dies young or is stricken with debilitating diseases, or why people who would be great parents are unable to bear children and those who shouldn't have any children have several.

Unfortunately, life doesn't start people out on the same playing field, and the key is to recognize that you have no control over those inequities. What you do have control over, however, is where you end up, and that is a direct result of how you choose to live your life and your response to life's inequities. Through determination and persistence, you can even the score or at least do your part to narrow the gap for yourself and for future generations of people of color. I also want you to take to heart the words of one of the best orators and the greatest civil rights activist who ever lived:

> *Whatever career you may choose for yourself—doctor, lawyer, teacher—let me propose an avocation to be pursued along with it. Become a dedicated fighter for civil rights. Make it a central part of your life. It will make you a better doctor, a better lawyer, a better teacher. It will enrich your spirit as nothing else possibly can. It will give you that rare sense of nobility that can only spring from love and selflessly helping your fellow man. (Martin Luther King, Jr., Speech Before the Youth March for Integrated Schools, April 18, 1959).*

This doesn't mean people won't deny you jobs, promotions, loans or other opportunities because of the color of your skin, or that while you are seeking to make humanity a better place, there won't be people seeking to undermine this very lesson. You may also have to work twice as hard to be successful simply because of the color of your skin. This will make you mad, and it should. I grant you, it is not right—it's downright unfortunate. However, through the anger, I want you to know you are so much more than any of that and destined to achieve a good deal in spite of all of that. Why? Because the enemy you know is a lot easier to defeat when you acknowledge who and what it is, and I want you to recognize life's inequities for what they are.

Once acknowledged, I want you to recognize your own value and capabilities and that neither injustice, nor inequity can stop you from being successful. Then I want you to move forward and narrow not only the inequities between you and the rest of the world but also do your part to narrow the inequities for your race. Draft a plan for what you want to achieve in life and start pursuing it. When Plan A doesn't work, go to Plan B; if Plan B doesn't work, go to C, and so forth. The key is to keep planning, to keep moving forward and to not be deterred. Remember, life's inequities and injustices remain inequities only to those who accept them.

Love Mom,

Mother of the Equalizers

There are only two lasting bequests we can hope to give our children. One is roots. The other is wings.

—Hodding Carter, Jr.

Lesson Five:
Character And Integrity Matter

o o o o o o o o o o o o o o o o o o o o o o o o o o o o o o

Our character is what we do when we think no one is looking.

—H. Jackson Brown, Jr.

Judge me, O Lord, according to my righteousness, and,…integrity that is in me.

—Psalms 7:8.

Dear Integrity Seekers:

I remember coming across a Chinese proverb: "Flies never visit an egg that has no crack." At the time, I thought that was the weirdest proverb I had ever read. Proverbs, after all, are supposed to imply some hidden wisdom, and I saw nothing wise about that particular proverb at the time.

Over time, however, this proverb has become the core of how I live my life and how I want you to live yours. What do an egg, a fly and a crack have in common you ask? To me, it's all about integrity and understanding. In essence, as long as you are solid at the core, neither flies nor anything else you abhor can break through. The Merriam-Webster dictionary defines integrity as a firm adherence to a code of especially moral or artistic values: INCORRUPTIBILITY. Yes, I know this sounds much easier than it is; nevertheless, you must strive for the moral ethical compass.

Case in point: When I was in fourth grade, my teacher, Ms. Baxter, asked me and three other girls to help her stock the class supply cabinet. On that occasion, the teacher also asked Tierra Bray, the toughest girl in the fourth grade, if not the entire school, to help too. When Ms. Baxter left the room for a few moments, Tierra capitalized on her absence and recruited several of her friends to steal some of the paper from the supply cabinet as I watched. They told me if Ms. Baxter asked, I should lie and say I brought the paper from home and gave it to them. They knew Ms. Baxter would believe me because I had had a reputation in that school, since kindergarten, as someone with integrity. Later that day, Ms. Barnes noticed the girls with the paper and asked where they got it from. They lied and told her that I gave it to them.

Out of fear, I confirmed their story. Truth is, at that time, I feared Tierra more than my conscience. As the day went on, the lie began to bother me. I was still a child, but school was the one place I felt valued because teachers and students respected me. I was smart and honorable, but in that instant I had lost my credibility. By the end of the day, I coudn't take it anymore and prepared to tell Ms. Baxter the truth.

When the bell rang to end the school day, I waited until all the kids left the room to tell Ms. Baxter I had lied to her. She thanked me, informed me she knew I had lied and stated she would confront the girls the next day. All night, I agonized over attending school. The next morning I feigned illness so I didn't have to go. Although I felt better about redeeming myself with Ms. Baxter, I knew that would be short-lived once Tierra saw me. After a few days, I returned to school. To my surprise, Tierra and the other girls ran to greet me. I learned that when Ms. Baxter confronted them, they took responsibility for the theft and admitted they had asked me to lie.

While that situation turned out well, I haven't always been so lucky. Take the incident involving Donise Smith when I was in the seventh grade. Donise, in those days, was considered mentally retarded; and as is typical of school-yard behavior, the other kids constantly taunted her. She and I, however, were good friends, even though I was ashamed to let anyone know.

One day, while hanging out with the "popular crowd," we started teasing Donise. Although I felt guilty, I joined the teasing too and called her "Retard" and "Slow Poke." Donise was hurt by my actions and challenged me to a fight in front of everyone. Although I didn't want to fight her, I felt compelled to do so because I couldn't let someone viewed as mentally inept beat me up. My friends in the popular crowd encouraged me to fight Donise and, like all friends in the hood, they swore they had my back.

Armed with this information, I prepared to fight Donise. At the end of the day, let's just say that she clobbered me, and not one of my supposed friends jumped in to save me from humiliation. Instead, they teased me about losing a fight to a mentally retarded person. I lost both the fight and one of my dearest friends because I chose popularity over friendship, even though I knew it was wrong.

These examples illustrate the lessons of personal integrity in my own life. They showed me the difference between right and wrong and taught me fairness, respect for others and listening to my inner voice. Most importantly, these experiences taught me that integrity matters, and that when you maintain your integrity, you always win.

While these experiences happened during my youth, the truth is, you will confront situations that challenge your integrity throughout your life. The extent to which you live with integrity will determine the quality of your life. You won't be able to control what people say, do or think of you. However, you can control whether integrity is a core value exemplified in your life. Other people, events and forces will seek to alter your integrity, but you and you alone ultimately control your personal integrity.

I must admit this isn't always an easy thing, because it's hard to go against the status quo and face ridicule. It's also hard to lose the love and companionship of friends and family. However, integrity demands that you speak your convictions beyond the circle of people with whom you share them. Miguel De Cervantes got it right when he said, "He who loses wealth loses much; he who loses a friend loses more; but he that loses his courage loses all." This is true.

When you sacrifice your integrity, you cease to be your authentic self. When you compromise your personal integrity because of peer pressure, fear or some personal or economic desire, it ultimately leads to failure and leaves you devastated in the long run. Integrity isn't something you demonstrate just when things are popular or agreeable to the masses. It's a behavior. A lifestyle. It's something you exercise wherever you are and whatever you're doing, even if the world disagrees with you.

I have yet to meet a person who can say he or she has demonstrated integrity 100 percent of the time. Even so, the challenge is to lessen the gap between your true moral compass and your daily behavior. A good way to do this is to establish a code of behavior which guides your actions and helps you maintain your integrity. This code can serve as a standard by which you assess your daily behavior to determine if it is reflective of your true moral compass. For example, if courage is a trait you value and believe is indicative of someone who lives his or her life with integrity, then ask whether your daily behavior is reflective of someone who shows courage. If not, ask how you can improve your daily behavior to be more in alignment with your true moral compass.

Here are some other things I think will help you live your life with integrity:

1. **Keep your word.** A key trait of a person who lives with integrity is whether that person keeps his or her word or promises. After all, your word is your bond, and integrity is an unwavering commitment to the promises you have made, unless they threaten the safety and health of yourself or others.

2. **Be truthful where it matters.** Sure, there will be occasions when you will tell a falsehood, like the existence of Santa Claus and the Tooth Fairy. However, always be truthful where it matters. Never tell people they're right when you believe they're wrong or that you agree when you disagree. Always speak up, because falsehoods about things that are core to your character or your value system will never allow you serenity.

3. **Listen to your inner voice.** If you ever knowingly say something or exhibit a behavior to be popular or for any other reason, that doesn't make you feel good, it's likely you have lost one of the most important things you have: your personal integrity. Every time you ignore your inner voice and fail to follow your own beliefs or values, you minimize your ability to live a happy, fruitful life. When you compromise to be agreeable, non-confrontational or popular, you give up some of your integrity.

4. **Find examples.** Seek out examples of people of integrity for your own inspiration and guidance. There are numerous examples of people discussed or mentioned in the media every day who demonstrated minimal integrity in their lives. This includes CEOs and officers of companies who squandered or stole their employees' pensions, as well as politicians who vote along party lines rather than voting their conscience just to remain in power. There are other examples of people involved in identity theft, or of people who murder, lie, steal and cheat and cause extreme havoc and chaos, not only for others but also for the world. However, there are good examples as well. Jesus is the ultimate model of integrity, and the Bible is filled with people of integrity such as Job, Isaiah, and Jeremiah. You will learn what constitutes integrity by seeking out examples of people who have demonstrated it and people who haven't.

It's my desire that you know this virtue and espouse it, because a person who lives without integrity is no person at all.

Love Mom,

Your Guiding Light

Lesson Six:
You Are Your Brother's Keeper

○ ○

The Hottest places in HELL are reserved for those who, in times of great moral crisis, maintain their neutrality.

—*Dante Alighieri*

The ultimate measure of a man is not where he stands in moments of comfort and convenience but where he stands at times of challenge and controversy.

—*Dr. Martin Luther King, Jr.*

Dear Men Down for the Cause:

One of the most important stories you will ever learn stems from the biblical account of two brothers, Cain and Abel. In that story, Cain killed his brother Abel because he envied him. After Cain murdered Abel, God asked where Abel was, and Cain replied, "I know not; Am I my brother's keeper?"

In a nutshell: Absolutely! In my opinion, Cain got it wrong, but his words, unfortunately, provide the framework for our world today. People seem unwilling to recognize the connectivity of humankind or to accept any responsibility for the welfare of other individuals in our society—our brothers in the extended sense of the term.

As African-American men, you need to know it isn't sufficient for only a few in our race to prosper. Over the last few decades, the African-American community has witnessed a constant deterioration of socio-economic conditions that have resulted in a devastating effect on our race. This includes a burgeoning concern over HIV and AIDS infections in our community, the number of female-headed households, black-on-black crime and the criminalization and rates of recidivism among African-Americans in the penal system.

No single factor explains the seriousness of the situation facing the African-American community. Racism, both overt and covert, poverty, single-family households and lack of jobs clearly contribute to the problem. However, I suspect some of it also stems from the total displacement of African values, which tend to espouse collective empowerment and uplift, with the more individualistic American values. Values such as, "It takes a village to raise a child," clearly recognize the connectivity of humankind and the role the community plays in the elevation and success of others. In contrast, the American concept of rugged individualism recognizes the individual as the sole source of his or her success. As such, the adherence to American values has caused African-Americans to fixate on the "me" rather than the "we," the result of which is prosperity for a few, leaving many in despair.

Now let me be clear. This doesn't mean the American values aren't important. They are, because they recognize the role individuals must play in ensuring their own success. So I don't want you to disregard the American values. Rather, I want you to find the balance between the me and the we and recognize that your success and the success of your children are connected to the success of others in our race.

Senator Barak Obama (D-Ill.) spoke to this point in his keynote address, *The Audacity of Hope*, at the Democratic National Convention in 2004. In that speech, he stated:

> If there's a child on the south side of Chicago who can't read, that matters to me, even if it's not my child. If there's a senior citizen somewhere who can't pay for their prescription and having to choose between medicine and the rent, that makes my life poorer, even if it's not my grandparent…It's that fundamental belief—I am my brother's keeper, I am my sister's keeper—that makes this country work. (Barak Obama, *Audacity of Hope*, Democratic National Convention, July 17, 2004).

Senator Obama's message gets to the point. It recognizes the collective, and I want you to as well. Therefore, I encourage you to do the following:

1. **Be the voice for others when they have none.** Whether you're the guy standing up to the bully on the block or a charismatic politician, take a stance, not only on behalf of yourself but also for others. Although many people choose not to get involved in the lives of others because of

fear, apathy or helplessness, I want you to recognize that it's important that you do get involved. Recognize that to serve as the voice of others who may not have any is a big deal, and it is important and more people should do it.

2. **Be a part of the village that raises a child.** Since you've arrived on the scene, I can certainly say, "Amen to that." In your lifetime, you will encounter more people and things than I ever dreamed possible. It's important that you recognize the circle of and connectivity of life. I hope you recognize the value of neighbors, the extended family and the community that helped to raise you, and their importance in helping you to raise your children. Throughout your life, I hope you choose to be an active rather than a passive participant in the lives of others. I hope you will be the neighbor who participates in the carpool, who watches out for the latchkey kid, who serves as a big brother or surrogate father to another kid in need of a role model or the man who mentors another individual at work.

3. **Blaze a trail.** Make a pathway for those who come behind you. I heard this continuously growing up and throughout my career in corporate America. But more importantly, we hope you recognize it as a value you learned at home. Many of the discussions around the dinner table and witnessed behaviors should be examples of how and what to do to ensure that your walk down a chosen path is a prosperous one, a path that will have implications for your children, your grandchildren, your great-grandchildren and, hopefully, your race.

In the end, there's a common thread running through all of this: the belief that what you do for yourself is done for the collective. It's also the recognition that the key to your prosperity and that of the African-American race is intertwined with the recognition that you are your brother's keeper and that is something to be appreciated, respected, and valued.

Love Mom,

Keeper of Brothers

Lesson Seven:
The True Measure Of A Man From A Woman's Perspective

o o o o o o o o o o o o o o o o o o o o o o o o o o o o o
Your faults as a son are my failures as a father.

—Marcus Aurelius to son Commodus
(in Gladiator, 2000)

Dear Beloved Sons:

At this age in my life, I've come to realize the greatest gift anyone can ever give you as an African-American man is to provide you an understanding of the concept of manhood. I know it may seem strange for a woman to espouse guidance on what constitutes the true measure of a man. I know these aren't things you thought you would ever hear from your mother. Well, you are, but only from the perspective of how you treat women. For me, this is important, because throughout your life society will bombard you with the belief that your value as a man is intertwined with sexual promiscuity and machoism. If I'm successful at nothing else, I hope I convince you that, for a woman, the true measure of a man lies in the love and respect he shows toward women and the value he places on family.

I remember going to a corner store in my neighborhood when I was young and encountering a crowd of people yelling and screaming and trying to stop an irate man from hitting his girlfriend. As they pulled him off her, he hurled every obscenity in the book at her. I entered the store (yes, I continued into the store because this was a typical scene in my neighborhood) and caught a glimpse of her. I watched as blood from a slight cut trickled down one side of her face, and tears down the other. I sensed her embarrassment over the situation, as well as her helplessness over loving a man who insisted on abusing her and disrespecting her at will. His actions clearly demonstrated he didn't respect or value her, and I turned away so as to not embarrass her any further.

When I exited the store, I saw the man standing outside, smoking a cigarette with his friends. I heard him say, "I can sleep with whoever I want. I told her a man is going to be a man. I'm the king of my house, and if she don't like it, the [expletive] can leave." His boys laughed and nodded their heads in agreement.

Although I didn't say anything to the man, I pitied him because he had confused manhood with disrespect and abuse. I knew his mother would be disappointed if she had witnessed his behavior, because I couldn't imagine any mother who would support this type of destructive behavior toward a woman. Although he insisted on acting like he was the king of his house, he had no realization that he was king because he lived with a queen. Rather, he believed he had earned the title because he had declared war on the queen, won the battle and made her his prisoner of war.

Many men don't realize that the title of king is an honor they earn, bestowed by those who love them and feel protected by them. It's not an absolute, automatic right. Even so, I could only pity the abusive man, because all my life I had seen young men criticized for respecting women and praised for denigrating them. It's the same praise system that rewards a man for having numerous kids with different women out of wedlock, for having multiple sex partners and for killing another man over something as simple as an accidental bump at a party or a pair of sneakers. It's popularized and reinforced every day by popular culture, in music and movies.

I tell you this not to scare or criticize you, but to prepare you to fight society's imposition of these beliefs on you. As your mother, I want you to know the true measure of a man, which can be seen in men who love and respect their women, their children and themselves. It can be seen in the man who is present when his children are born and remains a presence throughout their lives. Or, in the man who teaches his children to ride a bike or play football, or who treats his spouse or partner as an equal, and the man who works hard every day to support his family. These men are the ones worthy of being called kings. I hope throughout your life you learn:

1. **Respect for women.** I say it once, twice, three times and more, if necessary, that it's okay to respect women. Please open doors and pull out chairs for them. Buy them flowers and compliment them on how nice they look. This isn't weak, but respectful, and you will be the better for it.

2. **Never raise your hand to a woman.** If you ever get to the point in a relationship where you feel you need to abuse the person, simply leave. Terminate the relationship. Nothing ever justifies hitting a woman, and believe me, you will never recover or earn back your integrity or respect if you do this. Even worse, you will disappoint your mother, because she didn't raise you to abuse another human being.

3. **Realize that no means no.** A woman always has the right to say no, even if she said yes at first or had said yes on previous occasions. This is true whether she is dressed a certain way, led you on, or you bought her an expensive meal or a diamond ring or even after you're married to her. Remember, it is always her prerogative to say no or to change her mind at any given time, and only she has the right to choose to be intimate with you.

4. **Treat her as your equal.** Recognize that every woman you date, and particularly the one you marry, has her own opinions, her own thoughts and her own ideas. The point is not that you rule over her, but that you rule with her.

5. **Take care of your children.** Whether or not you and the mother of your children remain in a relationship, recognize that your kids are your kids and you are their father. Being a part of their lives is not optional. It's mandatory. They deserve it. More importantly, you deserve the privilege of raising them and watching them grow.

6. **Place popular culture in perspective.** Forget what you see in the rap videos or hear in songs. Never say or call a woman anything you wouldn't want someone to call your mother, sister or daughter. Believe me when I say words not only hurt, they also destroy. Use them carefully, and if you can't say anything nice, don't say anything at all!

Love Mom,

Woman Raising Real Men!

Lesson Eight:
A Penny Saved Is A Penny Earned

o o o o o o o o o o o o o o o o o o o o o o o o o o o o o o

I have enough money to last me the rest of my life, unless I buy something.

—Jackie Mason

Anyone who says money can't buy happiness just doesn't know where to shop.

—Bumper Sticker

Dear Budding Entrepreneurs:

Many people grow up with the dream of being rich. They envision money allowing them the opportunity to acquire luxurious items, such as a vacation home, a sports car and the ability to travel abroad. For many, however, the attainment of wealth will remain an unrealized dream.

Because of this, at some point in your life you are destined to hear someone say, "Money won't buy happiness," and "Money is the root of all evil." In some sense, these phrases are true. However, we live in a capitalistic society, the underpinning of which is that anyone can obtain financial freedom. Unfortunately, many African-Americans never learn the reality of getting and keeping money, because it's rarely discussed in our households or in the public schools.

My parents never spoke about money. After all, we were poor. The mere mention of money, other than to say, "I don't have any," was taboo. No one ever educated me on the importance of investments, savings, credit or acquiring assets. They certainly never discussed concepts such as wealth factors or the importance of reading business journals such as the *Wall Street Journal* or *Investors Business Daily* to stay informed. As a child, financial independence and economic freedom appeared illusive.

I'm not surprised. As a race, we are constantly bombarded with self-destructive, limiting thoughts about our ability to acquire wealth. We are often taught and we, in turn, often teach our children, that it takes money to make money and that social connections matter more than merit. Although these concepts are true to some extent, they shouldn't be limiting or defining, and they certainly aren't absolutes.

Many African-Americans born to parents with little money and no connections accept the belief that attaining wealth is impossible for them. Thus, they resign themselves to the notion that fancy cars, designer clothes and name-brand shoes are the closest they will get to owning anything of value. To them, these items become synonymous with the American Dream, and the concept of "having it all." This remains true even if attaining these things forces them into bankruptcy or a cycle of living from paycheck to paycheck. After all, why delay gratification today when you don't foresee wealth in your future?

We are also taught that money begets problems. I remember once saying I wanted to be wealthy, whereupon my uncle told me that people with money only had problems. I remember thinking that poor people had problems too, and that I would rather be a rich person with problems than a poor person with them.

Over the years, I have come to realize this mindset—that money begets problems—serves as a defense mechanism for individuals who cannot see the possibility of attaining wealth or financial independence. This excuses them from striving for financial freedom and makes them feel better about their current lot. Interestingly, I'm not sure if this mindset was instilled by the few wealthy people to make the masses feel complacent, or by the masses themselves so they would feel better that they haven't accumulated wealth.

Either way, it's a shame when you really think about it. John Mortimer, English barrister and writer, was correct when he said, "The worst fault of the working classes is telling their children they're not going to succeed, saying, 'There is life, but it's not for you.'"

Can you imagine saying this to your child? Yet millions of parents do it every day, intentionally or unintentionally, by infecting their children with such mind-limiting beliefs. These thoughts contrast with the reality that African-Americans are a wealthy race. According to a report released in 2004 by the Selig Center for Economic Growth at the University of Georgia's Terry College of Business entitled *The Multicultural Economy: 2004*, it was projected that the economic buying power of the African-American race would amount to more than $700 billion in 2004.

While many people challenge whether money buys happiness, no one disputes that the absence of money makes most people miserable and that money is a source of real power. Therefore, it becomes imperative that you understand the importance of money and its role in our society. I know you're thinking, easier said than done, and that many millionaires have inherited their wealth. No doubt this is the case, but the world is filled with many self-made millionaires who pulled themselves up by their own bootstraps, whether in entertainment, real estate or business. Consider Oprah Winfrey, talk show host, and Bob Johnson, founder of Black Entertainment Television. These people were successful because they believed anything possible.

Although the fundamentals of wealth accumulation weren't taught in my home, I certainly intend to teach them to you. I believe that wealth accumulation is possible and, like anything else, requires focus, dedication and discipline. As I see it, these are the major six cardinal rules for wealth accumulation:

1. **Set Goals.** It's impossible to achieve anything, particularly wealth attainment or financial independence, without setting goals, which are the roadmap for your success. Make sure, however, that your goals are measurable. It's not sufficient to say you want to be rich. This isn't measurable. Rather, say you want to acquire $5 million, $100 million or some specific number. The more definable the goal, the better you can strive to make it possible.

2. **Live below your means.** This is critical. No matter how much money you make, you will always be poor if your income is less than your expenses. Budgeting is critical. Prepare a budget and stick with it. I know this may be extremely difficult, considering that popular culture tends to advocate excess purchasing and frivolous spending. After all, I don't know of many R&B, rock or rap songs or movies that focus on entrepreneurship, financial independence and wealth factors. Those who acquire wealth or financial independence, however, understand this cardinal rule and use it to their advantage.

3. **Pay yourself first.** You will never attain financial independence if you pay all your bills and everyone else first. Make sure you put something aside for yourself every paycheck, no matter what else you have to pay. A good rule of thumb is to invest or save 10–15 percent of your net income. If you want to get ahead more quickly, save more. If you don't

have this much to save, save as much as you can because the goal is simply to start saving.

4. **Become financially literate.** Never become passive with your money. Sure, you may know the difference between a pair of Air Jordans and a pair of Reeboks, but I also want you to know the difference between stocks and bonds, a money market account and a certificate of deposit and other financial instruments. I want you to understand the terms return on investment, price-to-equity ratio and compound interest. Know what the federal reserve board does and what a 401(k) and Roth IRA are, because knowledge is power.

5. **Balance long-term saving and short-term spending.** Find a balance between planning for your future and immediate gratification. Both are important, and you won't be happy if you only do one. The key is to find the appropriate mixture that enables you to enjoy your life in the present while striving for future financial independence.

6. **Invest early and often.** This speaks to the time value of money. The earlier you invest, the sooner your money begins to work for you. You will achieve financial independence more quickly if you start saving and investing at 25 than you will if you start at 35.

In the end, remember, the key to attaining financial independence lies within yourself.

Love Mom,

Hoping You Achieve Financial Independence

Lesson Nine: Peer Pressure Will Bankrupt You

○ ○
The individual has always had to struggle to keep from being overwhelmed by the tribe. If you try it, you will be lonely often, and sometimes frightened. But no price is too high to pay for the privilege of owning yourself.

—Friedrich Nietzsche

Don't think you're on the right road just because it's a well-beaten path.

—Author Unknown

Dear Sons:

At some point in your life, you will be pushed by friends to smoke a cigarette or marijuana, throw a rock at a passing car or do something worse that you may not really want to do or you feel is inappropriate. This is peer pressure. It means being influenced by people your age or within your social group to do something you would not have done without their influence. Beloved sons, if there were anything more, excluding racism, that I wish I could shield you from, it would be peer pressure.

My grandmother's favorite saying, after "You don't believe fat meat is greasy," was "Peer pressure will bankrupt you." She believed peer pressure was the most dangerous thing that many young people faced. She believed the desire to be liked by friends could force young people to do things that led to their death, but most often left them bankrupt, either morally, financially, or both.

As my grandmother's saying makes clear, peer pressure often has a much greater influence over young people than even family or religion. It's easy to give into peer pressure because of curiosity, because everyone is doing it, or for the desire to be popular. No one wants to be made fun of, and everyone wants to be cool. As your mom, this concerns me because, believe it or not, I was young once. I understand that the desire to be accepted can be so strong that you may disobey me, toss your personal convictions aside and even risk your life, intentionally or unintentionally.

I remember a time when a good friend of mine, Claudia, suggested we burn some bags of trash lying beside our house. We were just curious about fire. What kid isn't? Although I didn't really want to burn the trash bags, because my mom always told me not to play with fire, I did it out of fear of being teased and called a baby. You see, Claudia was cool, and because of my desire to be cool, I agreed. We lit the fire, but before we could extinguish it, it became uncontrollable and we could not stop it. As the fire grew, Claudia and I became scared and ran.

Luckily for us, my older cousin spotted the fire and came over to assist. He found a water hose and put the fire out before a catastrophe occured. Although I got severely disciplined for my behavior, I felt ashamed because I realized I had almost burned down my family's house simply to be cool. Believe me when I say, no amount of popularity could have cured that feeling.

Although I didn't learn my lesson about peer pressure immediately, I did eventually. One time I went shopping with my friends Debra and Janee, who wanted to steal a shirt from a store. They encouraged me to steal one so that we could all dress alike. I felt uncomfortable and refused to steal the shirt. I left the store, even though they teased me. They did steal the shirt, but I felt good about my refusal to not participate in something I knew was wrong.

In both situations, I was forced to make my own decision about right and wrong. It wasn't easy to do. Although Debra and Janee stopped being my friends over the incident, I felt good about my decision. I learned that the feeling you get from living your life right is greater than the one you get from being cool, even if your decision is unpopular.

As an African-American man, your ability to stand strong in the face of peer pressure will be constantly tested. Why? For some reason, the lack of economic and social advantages forces many men into dangerous situations with their peers. For example, gangs take on greater importance and priority in the lives of many inner-city youth. Men who seek education or success are sometimes taunted by their peers as being or acting "white" or even nerdy, and such labels are almost always a sign of certain social death for youth. This type of pressure can cause even the strongest person to conform and become involved in bad situations.

As you grow older, you too will be faced with challenging decisions. They aren't always black or white. Some decisions may pose serious moral dilemmas, such as whether you should steal, have sex before you're ready or lie to your parents. At other times, peer pressure will force you to choose between being popular or smart, right or wrong, or between life and death.

Peer pressure is hard to resist, but because of its consequences, you must pay attention to your own feelings about what you believe is the right course of action. Your inner strength and self-confidence will help you to stand firm and walk away or else the desire to be cool or accepted by your peers will surely bankrupt you.

Love Mom,

The Woman Who Hopes You Don't Go Broke

Lesson Ten:
Success Does Not Equal Acting White

Children can't achieve unless we raise their expectations and turn off the television sets and eradicate the slander that says a black youth with a book is acting white.

—Sen. Barak Obama, (D-Ill.), Democratic National Convention, 2004

There are many who are living far below their possibilities because they are continually handing over their individualities to others. Do you want to be a power in the world? Then be yourself. Be true to the highest within your soul and then allow yourself to be governed by no customs or conventionalities or arbitrary man-made rules that are not founded on principle.

—Ralph Waldo Trine, author of In Tune With the Infinite and The Greatest Thing Ever Known

Dear Future Successful Men:

One of the hardest lessons I ever had to learn was that it was acceptable to want an education. Although the desire for an education may seem like a given, for many youths growing up in my neighborhood it was not an easy option. Believe it or not, every day during my sophomore year of high school, kids teased and chided me for not only attending school but also for being too smart at school.

In truth, I believe I could have accepted the chiding had the kids called me a nerd. Instead they told me I was "acting white" and called me everything from a "sell-out" to a "white girl." I'd be lying if I told you it didn't hurt, because as an African-American, nothing hurts more than to hear others say you have shunned and shamed your race. This is particularly true and disheartening when you believe you are only striving for upward mobility.

I can't tell you the number of times I snuck off to the school library or stayed up late at night to do homework so no one would see me studying and trying to learn. I also can't tell you how many times I pretended to be stupid to stop the teasing.

That was 15 years ago. Unfortunately, things have only gotten worse today. In fact, at some point in your life you may also be labeled as "acting white" or called a "sell-out" on your quest to become educated, or merely because you're successful. To me, "acting white" means that a person of color is emulating white culture by imitating a behavior deemed indicative of that culture. Although the teasing hurts, I want you to hold your head high. There is no shame in wanting to be educated or successful. It's stupid to believe that the Caucasian race holds a monopoly on education, reading or anything else associated with success.

While many people may view the teasing as a sign of anti-intellectualism on the part of African-American youth, I disagree. I believe the abhorrence of education serves as a defense mechanism for those who have an innate sense of inferiority and who fear they aren't intelligent. These slurs, while unacceptable, in many cases, are merely an attempt to reclaim power and are the only recourse for many of them.

Although I eventually managed to withstand the harassment, lots of African-American youth aren't able to and are pressured by their peers to act as if they lack intelligence. This is true even though they are smart. I know of many examples of children who are intelligent but who refuse to show it because of this counterculture that says it's cool to be stupid. Of course, this is ridiculous because these same individuals often find out later that it's not cool to stand on street corners with no job, no legitimate means of support and no viable future.

Unfortunately, many youth don't understand, because few adults stand up to counter this negative message. I honestly can't think of one adult in my community or in the village of people who raised me who told me that getting an education was a priority, or who did anything to stymie the teasing I faced.

While this counterculture is an issue the African-American community must continue to grapple with, I want to make clear to you that education is a priority, and it is of paramount importance. It is a non-negotiable part of your future. It is the key to power, and it will make or break you. This is so even though people will attempt to thwart your efforts to obtain education or your success by hurling hurtful words at you, such as telling you you're acting white.

You need to know, however, that success and education are no longer reserved for Whites Only. Many of your ancestors fought to be educated. History is replete with examples of African-Americans who were killed for wanting to learn to read and write, or who died trying to integrate schools and universities. They would have found criticism of African-Americans seeking to be educated very disheartening.

If no other adult makes this clear, I want to make certain that you hear it from me: seeking to learn and obtaining an education are good things. So while in some circles it may be cool to be stupid, in my circle, it's always stupid to be uneducated. And I know I'm not raising stupid boys.

Love Mom,

The Woman Who Knows Education Is the Key to the Future

Lesson Eleven: Put God First

○ ○
But Jesus beheld them, and said unto them, With men this is impossible; but with God all things are possible.

—Matthew 19:26, King James Version

Dear God's Children:

I was definitely raised in the church. I have fond memories of attending Vacation Bible School, belonging to youth choir, memorizing the books of the Bible, giving Easter and Christmas speeches and attending regional conferences in nearby cities. Every Sunday morning, hymns flowed out the church's front door, and our minister always gave a sermon that combined the teachings of God with the realities of life. The church women, along with my mom, helped raise me. From them, I've learned to sit up straight, not to chew gum in formal settings, to be a good Christian, that the shield is mightier than the sword, that what doesn't kill us only makes us stronger and that God doesn't like ugly.

The church has always been a permanent structure in the African-American community. During slavery and through America's tumultuous race relations, the church has served as the place the African-American community could call home. It not only served as a place of worship, but also as a place of community. At and through church, we interacted with others in our community, got involved in politics, learned domestication, found respect for our fellow man, met and married our spouses, baptized our children and gave our lives over to God.

As a child, I fought going to church. However, as an adult, I have come to appreciate the comfort of knowing I never walk alone and the overwhelming devotion to a higher power that the church instilled in me. I've never really thought about it, but I guess I am a spiritual person. I now put into practice all the things I've read, witnessed in the lives of others and that have been instilled in me. When I look back on difficult situations I've encountered in my life, I know it had to be God that got me over it, under it or through it, and that in some circumstances he even carried me. I know I have made it this far because of my prayers and my family's prayers, asking God to watch over me.

Even though I don't get to church as often as I should, nothing prevents me from acknowledging and worshipping God every day, expressing my gratitude for the numerous blessings he has given me and for always knowing that I'm his child. In the end, we are products of our history and learning. This is certainly one legacy I hope to pass on to you.

In today's society, it may not seem cool to worship and praise God. However, I assure you there is nothing more hip or cool than being spiritually connected to an awesome, powerful God, the creator of life, heaven and earth. It's truly a blessing to know God in such a spiritual way. God's love, and your love for him, is a legacy that will prepare you for life's challenges and provide you with an armor so strong that nothing will stand in the way of your true greatness, not to mention all that life will throw your way.

Here are some things I know for sure, because of my continued faith in God. I hope you will learn:

1. **God wants you to prosper.** God created a world of abundance. I believe in a good God that wants you to have a wonderful life. While most people associate prosperity with money, I want you to know that the prosperity God wants for you is so much more than money. It's prosperity with regard to your quality of life, and it covers all your needs from health to joy to peace to love.

2. **God doesn't give you more than you can handle.** He didn't bring you into this world so that you would suffer. When you encounter a situation that seems too much, pray for guidance, have faith and wait for instruction. You will find God always makes a way, and the difficult situation you thought impossible becomes resolvable and bearable or at a minimum, he brings you through it stronger than you were.

3. **God will give blessings to you, if he trusts he can give blessings *through* you.** In other words, be a good steward. Help those in need. Make charity and philanthropy and pure kindness core to your existence. Blessings don't flow from what you receive. They are the result of what you give and how that makes you feel.

4. **As long as you believe there is a God, then there is always hope.**
5. **Don't call on God only during bad times, but also in good times.** Believe me, you need him more in the good times than the bad, because it is during good times that you can lose your way, and that is when you need his love and guidance to sustain and support you.
6. **Don't be envious of another's good fortune.** Good fortune for anyone is to be welcomed because their success is ultimately your success. This goes hand-in-hand in recognizing the collective power of the we and not just fixating on the me.
7. **Pray through your pain.** Prayer is powerful and it heals. It's also your communication vehicle with God so use it often.

As I continue to live and grow in my relationship with God, the one thing I hope to pass on to you is to put God first and foremost in everything you do. I'll always be praying for you.

Love Mom,

Woman Who Will Always Be Praying For You

Afterword

I don't profess to be an academic, a sociologist, a psychologist or an individual of any of those learned professions, and I didn't write this book from that perspective. I am a mother first and foremost. As a mother, I understand that we live in uncertain times and that life has gotten much tougher for our youth. When I wrote this book, I didn't have only my sons on my mind but also future generations of young African-American men. The plight of many African-American men, particularly those in the inner-cities across America, weigh heavily on my heart. Their plight is an arduous one and it requires a good deal of parenting. I hope African-American mothers will use the lessons in this book either as a guide to teach their own children or at least as topics of discussions. As mothers, our job is difficult. It's my sincere hope that this book has made that job easier in some way.

Selected Bibliography

Books

The following books were used in writing Lesson One.

Aldred, Cyril. *Akhenaten: King of Egypt*. New York: Thames & Hudson, Inc., 1988.

Asante, Molefi Kete. *The Egyptian Philosphers: Ancient African Voices from Imhotep to Akhenaten*. Chicago: African American Images, 2000.

Brooks, Lester. *Great Civilizations of Ancient Africa*. New York: Atheneum, 1971.

Clayton, Peter A. *Chronicles of the Pharaohs: The Reign-By-Reign Record of the Rulers and Dynasties of Ancient Egypt*. New York: Thames & Hudson, Ltd, 1994.

Corbin, Raymond M. *1999 Facts About Blacks, 2nd Edition A Sourcebook of African-American Achievement*. Maryland: Madison Books, 1997.

Gates, Dr. Henry Louis. *Little Known Black History Facts*, McDonald's Corporation, 2000.

McKissack, Patricia. *Nzingha: Warrior Queen of Matamba, Angola, Africa, 1595 (The Royal Diaries)*. New York: Scholastic Inc, 2000.

Redford, Donald B. *Akhenaten: The Heretic King*. New Jersey: Princeton University Press, 1984.

Reeves, Nicholas. *Ancient Egypt: The Great Discoveries* . New York: Thames & Hudson, Ltd., 2000.

Rogers, J.A. *World's Great Men of Color*. New York: Touchstone, Revised Reprint Edition, 1996, Vol. 1.

Schwaller de Lubicz, R. A. *The Temples of Karnak*. Vermont: Inner Traditions, 1999.

978-0-595-39644-3
0-595-39644-5

Printed in the United States
127966LV00004B/448-555/A